Dedication

To my daughter, Jean, who rescued Parker, and to my wife, Pat, who gave her a home. You brought more than a little dog into our lives. You brought us laughter, licks, and love, the kind of love that only Parker could give.

Parker
The Homeless Dog

Written By Bob Merz
Illustrated By Debbie J Hefke

Ooh, I looove my bed. So soft and comfy. In my bed I dream about playing Fetch and Chase Me with my family.

Fetch

Chase

But, it's time to get up and. . .

Oh yeah, I slept under a car again. That's what homeless puppies do. But every night, I dream of having a home and family of my very own. I would love to have a name, too.

But wait. Behind the school parking lot, the cafeteria dumpster has. . .

TACOS! Munch, munch. Sooo good, but a little warm. **REALLY** warm. No,

REALLY, REALLY HOT!

I run across the parking lot looking for water – sprinting back and forth, up and down, and round and round, until. . .

A puddle! Slurp, Slurp, Lap, Lap.
My face gets all drippy wet, but I don't
care.

AAAH!

Suddenly, a car drives in, and a lady gets out. Maybe she'll wanna take me home. I dance my happy dance and smile my biggest smiley smile.

"Ugh, go away, you hairless stray mutt," she yells. Hey lady, I'm not a stray. I'm homeless! And I'm losing my hair 'cause I'm starving, **GET IT?**

Then a man sees me. Maybe he'll take
me home. I dance and smile again.

But he kicks at me.

So I scamper under a car to hide.

DUDE, WHAT'S WRONG WITH YOU?

Geez, some people are so mean. That makes me so mad, but mostly sad. I feel like crying but, I fall asleep instead.

RIIIIIIING! What was. . .
BANG!

Oh man, I gotta find a home.

Hey. . . Maybe those kids on the playground will take me home.

I dance my happy dance and smile my smiley smile.

A little girl says, "This puppy looks funny."
Funny, what's so funny? "Yeah," says a boy,
"This mutt's going bald, **ha—ha**."

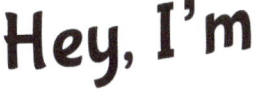

Hey, I'm no mutt! And what's bald anyway?

The biggest boy throws a rock at me. Luckily,
the kid can't throw straight, and misses.

Just then, a young teacher walks up and scolds the kids for being mean to me. "We're sorry Miss Jean," the kid's say, looking sooo guilty. She marches them off the playground.

But she gives me a big smile! I like this teacher, Jean!

I'm cute, I dance, and I give smiley smiles. What's not to like, ya know? I'm a tough puppy girl, but very sad this time, so I cry myself to sleep.

RIIIIIIING!

Ah man! What's with those stupid bells?

All the kids are getting in cars and buses. The mean lady is back, and she's talking to a big man with a gray truck, a stick and a net.

YIKES! A dogcatcher. I hear dogcatchers take puppies away. . . Forever!

The dogcatcher starts walking towards me, and then he runs. So I run, fast!

YOU'RE NOT CATCHING ME, BUDDY!

I run back and forth, up and down, and round and round, until huffing and puffing, the dogcatcher stops. "I'll get you, mutt!" he yells.

He finally catches me in his net.

I yelp my loudest puppy yelp —

YIP, YIP, YIP!

But he laughs, looking at me with scary, mean eyes.

Nice teacher Jean runs up to the dogcatcher.

"Excuse me, sir, that puppy belongs to me."

"Oh no she doesn't," says the mean lady. "Oh **YES** she does," says teacher Jean. "She is mine, this is her collar, and her name is, uh. . . Parker!"

WHAT? My name is Parker? That's a cool name!

Teacher Jean puts the collar on me, and it feels so good. . . Like love.

"C'mon, Parker," she says. We walk right past the dogcatcher and mean old lady.

Now how cool is that?

Teacher Jean takes me to her car. "Parker, let's go home!"

I jump and **BANG** my head on the dashboard. But that's okay, 'cause it's a **HAPPY HURT!** She's gonna take me home? She's the best!

As we drive away, I gaze at teacher Jean with my all-time biggest smiley smile.

My name is **Parker**, and I'm going home!

The End

Teacher Jean was so kind and rescued me. Do you know why? 'Cause she felt something deep inside her heart – she felt empathy. Teacher Jean wondered what it would be like to be homeless like me. She wondered what it would be like to be hungry, with no home, living under cars, and with no one to love her. She felt empathy and so she took me home to love and care for me. See if you can feel like someone else is feeling. See if you can feel empathy for someone, or for an animal.

Love, Parker

www.ingramcontent.com/pod-product-compliance
Lightning Source LLC
Chambersburg PA
CBHW041435120626
46547CB00002B/220